Sonnets
from the
Portuguese

Elizabeth Barrett Browning

Running Press
Philadelphia, Pennsylvania

A Running Press Miniature Edition

Copyright © 1989 by Running Press. Printed in Singapore.
All rights reserved under the Pan-American
and International Copyright Conventions.

This book may not be reproduced in whole or in part in any
form or by any means, electronic or mechanical, including
photocopying, recording, or by any information storage or
retrieval system now known or hereafter invented, without
written permission from the publisher.

Canadian representatives: General Publishing Co., Ltd., 30
Lesmill Road, Don Mills, Ontario M3B 2T6.

International representatives: Worldwide Media Services, Inc.,
115 East Twenty-third Street, New York, New York 10010

9 8 7 6 5 4 3 2 1
Digit on the right indicates the number of this printing.
Library of Congress Catalog Card Number:
88–43555   ISBN 0–89471–718–9

This book may be ordered by mail from the publisher. Please
include $2.50 for postage. But try your bookstore first! Running
Press Book Publishers, 125 South Twenty-second Street,
Philadelphia, Pennsylvania 19103

INTRODUCTION

These poems poured from the soul of a woman whose life was transformed by a most improbable love.

In 1845, Elizabeth Barrett, a well-known Victorian poet, was a housebound invalid nearly forty years old. A fan letter from a 33-year-old aspiring poet, Robert Browning, commenced a correspondence that quickly kindled to love, although the two did not meet face-fo-face for months. When Barrett's tyrannical father forbid her to marry, she found the strength to elope with Browning to Italy, where they lived happily in semi-exile until her death in 1861.

Robert Browning's nickname for Elizabeth was "the Portuguese," referring to a character in her poem "Catarina to Camoens." Writing this sequence of highly private sonnets about her astonishing love affair, she used that name, hoping to disguise the verses as a translation. But her passion shines through, making these her finest poems—and, indeed, some of the greatest love poems ever written.

F thought once how Theocritus
  had sung

Of the sweet years, the dear and wished for
  years,

Who each one in a gracious hand appears

To bear a gift for mortals, old or young:

And, as I mused it in his antique tongue,

I saw, in gradual vision through my tears,

The sweet, sad years, the melancholy years,

Those of my own life, who by turns had
  flung

A shadow across me. Straightway I was
   'ware,

So weeping, how a mystic Shape did move

Behind me, and drew me backward by the
   hair;

And a voice said in mastery, while I
   strove, . . .

'Guess now who holds thee?'—'Death,' I
   said. But, there,

The silver answer rang, . . . 'Not Death, but
   Love.'

ut only three in all God's universe

Have heard this word thou hast said,—
    Himself, beside

Thee speaking, and me listening! and
    replied

One of us . . . that was God, . . . and laid the
    curse

So darkly on my eyelids, as to amerce

My sight from seeing thee,—that if I had
    died,

The deathweights, placed there, would
    have signified

Less absolute exclusion. 'Nay' is worse

From God than from all others, O my
   friend!

Men could not part us with their worldly
   jars,

Nor the seas change us, nor the tempests
   bend;

Our hands would touch for all the
   mountain-bars,

And, heaven being rolled between us at the
   end,

We should but vow the faster for the stars.

_U_nlike are we, unlike, O princely
   Heart!

Unlike our uses and our destinies.

Our ministering two angels look surprise

On one another, as they strike athwart

Their wings in passing. Thou, bethink
   thee, art

A guest for queens to social pageantries,

With gages from a hundred brighter eyes

Than tears even can make mine, to play thy
   part

Of chief musician. What hast *thou* to do

With looking from the lattice-lights at me,

A poor, tired, wandering singer, singing through
The dark, and leaning up a cypress tree?

The chrism is on thine head,—on mine, the dew,—

And Death must dig the level where these agree.

Thou hast thy calling to some palace-floor,

Most gracious singer of high poems! where

The dancers will break footing, from the care

Of watching up thy pregnant lips for more.

And dost thou lift this house's latch too poor

For hand of thine? and canst thou think and bear

To let thy music drop here unaware

In folds of golden fulness at my door?

Look up and see the casement broken in,
The bats and owlets builders in the roof!
My cricket chirps against thy mandolin.
Hush, call no echo up in further proof
Of desolation! there's a voice within
That weeps. . .as thou must sing. . .alone,
   aloof.

lift my heavy heart up solemnly,

As once Electra her sepulchral urn,

And, looking in thine eyes, I overturn

The ashes at thy feet. Behold and see

What a great heap of grief lay hid in me,

And how the red wild sparkles dimly burn

Through the ashen greyness. If thy foot in
scorn

Could tread them out to darkness utterly,

It might be well perhaps. But if instead

Thou wait beside me for the wind to blow

The grey dust up, . . . those laurels on thine
head,

O my Belovèd, will not shield thee so,

That none of all the fires shall scorch and
shred

The hair beneath. Stand further off then!
go.

o from me. Yet I feel that I shall stand
Henceforward in thy shadow. Nevermore
Alone upon the threshold of my door
Of individual life, I shall command
The uses of my soul, nor lift my hand
Serenely in the sunshine as before,
Without the sense of that which I forbore, . . .
Thy touch upon the palm. The widest land

Doom takes to part us, leaves thy heart in
    mine
With pulses that beat double. What I do
And what I dream include thee, as the wine
Must taste of its own grapes. And when I
    sue
God for myself, He hears that name of
    thine,
And sees within my eyes the tears of two.

*T*he face of all the world is
    changed, I think,

Since first I heard the footsteps of thy soul

Move still, oh, still, beside me, as they stole

Betwixt me and the dreadful outer brink

Of obvious death, where I, who thought to
    sink,

Was caught up into love, and taught the
    whole

Of life in a new rhythm. The cup of dole

God gave for baptism, I am fain to drink,

And praise its sweetness, Sweet, with thee
    anear.

The names of country, heaven, are changed
    away

For where thou art or shalt be, there or
    here;

And this . . . this lute and song . . . loved
    yesterday,

(The singing angels know) are only dear

Because thy name moves right in what they
    say.

hat can I give thee back, O liberal
And princely giver, who hast brought the
    gold
And purple of thine heart, unstained,
    untold,
And laid them on the outside of the wall
For such as I to take or leave withal,
In unexpected largesse? am I cold,
Ungrateful, that for these most manifold
High gifts, I render nothing back at all?

Not so; not cold,—but very poor instead.
Ask God who knows. For frequent tears
    have run
The colours from my life, and left so dead
And pale a stuff, it were not fitly done
To give the same as pillow to thy head.
Go farther! let it serve to trample on.

an it be right to give what I can give?

To let thee sit beneath the fall of tears

As salt as mine, and hear the sighing years

Re-sighing on my lips renunciative

Through those infrequent smiles which fail to live

For all thy adjurations? O my fears,

That this can scarce be right! We are not peers,

So to be lovers; and I own, and grieve,

That givers of such gifts as mine are, must

Be counted with the ungenerous. Out, alas!

I will not soil thy purple with my dust,

Nor breathe my poison on thy
    Venice-glass,

Nor give thee any love . . . which were
    unjust.

Beloved, I only love thee! let it pass.

*Y*et, love, mere love, is beautiful
    indeed

And worthy of acceptation. Fire is bright,

Let temple burn, or flax; an equal light

Leaps in the flame from cedar-plank or
    weed

And love is fire; and when I say at need

I love thee . . . mark! . . . I love thee! . . . in thy
    sight

I stand transfigured, glorified aright,

With conscience of the new rays that
    proceed

Out of my face toward thine. There's noth-
    ing low

In love, when love the lowest: meanest
    creatures

Who love God, God accepts while loving
    so.

And what I *feel*, across the inferior features

Of what I *am*, doth flash itself, and show

How that great work of Love enhances
    Nature's.

nd therefore if to love can be
  desert,

I am not all unworthy. Cheeks as pale

As these you see, and trembling knees that
  fail

To bear the burden of a heavy heart,—

This weary minstrel-life that once was girt

To climb Aornus, and can scarce avail

To pipe now 'gainst the valley nightingale

A melancholy music,—why advert

To these things? O Belovèd, it is plain
I am not of thy worth nor for thy place!
And yet, because I love thee, I obtain
From that same love this vindicating grace,
To live on still in love, and yet in vain, . . .
To bless thee, yet renounce thee to thy
    face.

*F*ndeed this very love which is my
   boast,

And which, when rising up from breast to
   brow,

Doth crown me with a ruby large enow

To draw men's eyes and prove the inner
   cost, . . .

This love even, all my worth, to the
   uttermost,

I should not love withal, unless that thou

Hadst set me an example, shown me how,

When first thine earnest eyes with mine
   were crossed,

And love called love. And thus, I cannot
    speak

Of love even, as a good thing of my own:

Thy soul hath snatched up mine all faint
    and weak,

And placed it by thee on a golden throne,—

And that I love (O soul, we must be meek!)

Is by thee only, whom I love alone.

And wilt thou have me fashion into speech

The love I bear thee, finding words enough,

And hold the torch out, while the winds are rough,

Between our faces, to cast light on each?—

I drop it at thy feet. I cannot teach

My hand to hold my spirit so far off

From myself...me...that I should bring thee proof

In words, of love hid in me out of reach.

Nay, let the silence of my womanhood
Commend my woman-love to thy belief,—
Seeing that I stand unwon, however wooed,
And rend the garment of my life, in brief,
By a most dauntless, voiceless fortitude,
Lest one touch of this heart convey its grief.

*F*f thou must love me, let it be for nought

Except for love's sake only. Do not say

'I love her for her smile . . . her look . . . her way

Of speaking gently, . . . for a trick of thought

That falls in well with mine, and certes brought

A sense of pleasant ease on such a day'—

For these things in themselves, Belovèd, may

Be changed, or change for thee,—and love, so wrought,

May be unwrought so. Neither love me for

Thine own dear pity's wiping my cheeks
    dry,—

A creature might forget to weep, who bore

Thy comfort long, and lose thy love
    thereby!

But love me for love's sake, that evermore

Thou may'st love on, through love's
    eternity.

ccuse me not, beseech thee, that I
wear

Too calm and sad a face in front of thine;

For we two look two ways, and cannot shine

With the same sunlight on our brow and
hair.

On me thou lookest, with no doubting
care,

As on a bee shut in a crystalline;

Since sorrow hath shut me safe in love's
divine,

And to spread wing and fly in the outer air

Were most impossible failure, if I strove
To fail so. But I look on thee . . . on thee . . .
Beholding, besides love, the end of love,
Hearing oblivion beyond memory;
As one who sits and gazes from above,
Over the rivers to the bitter sea.

nd yet, because thou overcomest so,

Because thou art more noble and like a king,

Thou canst prevail against my fears and fling

Thy purple round me, till my heart shall grow

Too close against thine heart henceforth to know

How it shook when alone. Why, conquering

May prove as lordly and complete a thing

In lifting upward, as in crushing low!

And as a vanquished soldier yields his
sword

To one who lifts him from the bloody
earth,

Even so, Beloved, I at last record,

Here ends my strife. If *thou* invite me forth,

I rise above abasement at the word.

Make thy love larger to enlarge my worth.

*M*y poet, thou canst touch on all the notes

God set between His After and Before,

And strike up and strike off the general roar

Of the rushing worlds a melody that floats

In a serene air purely. Antidotes

Of medicated music, answering for

Mankind's forlornest uses, thou canst pour

From thence into their ears. God's will devotes

Thine to such ends, and mine to wait on
    thine.

How, Dearest, wilt thou have me for most
    use?

A hope, to sing by gladly?. . .or a fine

Sad memory, with thy songs to interfuse?

A shade, in which to sing. . .of palm or
    pine?

A grave, on which to rest from singing?
    Choose.

I never gave a lock of hair away
To a man, Dearest, except this to thee,
Which now upon my fingers thoughtfully,
I ring out to the full brown length and say
'Take it.' My day of youth went yesterday;
My hair no longer bounds to my foot's glee,
Nor plant I it from rose or myrtle-tree,
As girls do, any more: It only may

Now shade on two pale cheeks, the mark of tears,

Taught drooping from the head that hangs aside

Through sorrow's trick. I thought the funeral-shears

Would take this first, but Love is justified,—

Take it thou, . . . finding pure, from all those years,

The kiss my mother left here when she died.

The soul's Rialto hath its
merchandise;

I barter curl for curl upon that mart,

And from my poet's forehead to my heart

Receive this lock which outweighs
argosies,—

As purply black, as erst to Pindar's eyes

The dim purpureal tresses gloomed athwart

The nine white Muse-brows. For this coun-
terpart, . . .

The bay-crown's shade, Beloved, I surmise,

XIX

Still lingers on thy curl, it is so black!
Thus, with a fillet of smooth-kissing breath,
I tie the shadow safe from gliding back,
And lay the gift where nothing hindereth;
Here on my heart, as on thy brow, to lack
No natural heat till mine grows cold in
     death.

eloved, my Belovèd, when I think

That thou wast in the world a year ago,

What time I sat alone here in the snow

And saw no footprint, heard the silence sink

No moment at thy voice, but, link by link,

Went counting all my chains as if that so

They never could fall off at any blow

Struck by thy possible hand, . . .why, thus I drink

XX

Of life's great cup of wonder! Wonderful,
Never to feel thee thrill the day or night
With personal act or speech,—nor ever cull
Some prescience of thee with the blossoms
    white
Thou sawest growing! Atheists are as dull,
Who cannot guess God's presence out of
    sight.

Say over again, and yet once over
again,

That thou dost love me. Though the word
repeated

Should seem 'a cuckoo-song,' as thou dost
treat it,

Remember, never to the hill or plain,

Valley and wood, without her
cuckoo-strain,

Comes the fresh Spring in all her green
completed.

Belovèd, I, amid the darkness greeted

By a doubtful spirit-voice, in that doubt's
pain

XXI

Cry... 'Speak once more...thou lovest!'
Who can fear

Too many stars, though each in heaven
shall roll,

Too many flowers, though each shall crown
the year?

Say thou dost love me, love me, love
me—toll

The silver iterance!—only minding, Dear,

To love me also in silence with thy soul.

*W*hen our two souls stand up erect and strong,

Face to face, silent, drawing nigh and nigher,

Until the lengthening wings break into fire

At either curved point,—what bitter wrong

Can the earth do to us, that we should not long

Be here contented? Think. In mounting higher,

The angels would press on us and aspire

To drop some golden orb of perfect song

XXII

Into our deep, dear silence. Let us stay
Rather on earth, Belovèd,—where the unfit
Contrarious moods of men recoil away
And isolate pure spirits, and permit
A place to stand and love in for a day,
With darkness and the death-hour round-
      ing it.

s it indeed so? If I lay here dead,

Would'st thou miss any life in losing mine?

And would the sun for thee more coldly
shine

Because of grave-damps falling round my
head?

I marvelled, my Belovèd, when I read

Thy thought so in the letter. I am thine—

But . . . so much to thee? Can I pour thy
wine

While my hands tremble? Then my soul,
instead

XXIII

Of dreams of death, resumes life's lower
range.

Then, love me, Love! look on
me . . . breathe on me!

As brighter ladies do not count it strange,

For love, to give up acres and degree,

I yield the grave for thy sake, and exchange

My near sweet view of Heaven, for earth
with thee!

*L*et the world's sharpness, like a
   clasping knife,

Shut in upon itself and do no harm

In this close hand of Love, now soft and
   warm,

And let us hear no sound of human strife

After the click of the shutting. Life to life—

I lean upon thee, Dear, without alarm,

And feel as safe as guarded by a charm

Against the stab of worldlings, who if rife

XXIV

Are weak to injure. Very whitely still

The lilies of our lives may reassure

Their blossoms from their roots, accessible

Alone to heavenly dews that drop not
fewer,

Growing straight, out of man's reach, on
the hill.

God only, who made us rich, can make us
poor.

A heavy heart, Belovèd, have I
  borne

From year to year until I saw thy face,

And sorrow after sorrow took the place

Of all those natural joys as lightly worn

As the stringèd pearls, each lifted in its turn

By a beating heart at dance-time. Hopes
  apace

Were changed to long despairs, till God's
  own grace

Could scarcely lift above the world forlorn

XXV

My heavy heart. Then *thou* didst bid me
    bring
And let it drop adown thy calmly great
Deep being! Fast it sinketh, as a thing
Which its own nature doth precipitate,
While thine doth close above it, mediating
Betwixt the stars and the unaccomplished
    fate.

F lived with visions for my company

Instead of men and women, years ago,

And found them gentle mates, nor thought to know

A sweeter music than they played to me.

But soon their trailing purple was not free

Of this world's dust, their lutes did silent grow,

And I myself grew faint and blind below

Their vanishing eyes. Then THOU didst come...to be,

XXVI

Belovèd, what they seemed. Their shining
    fronts,

Their songs, their splendours (better, yet
    the same,

As river-water hallowed into fonts),

Met in thee, and from out thee overcame

My soul with satisfaction of all wants:

Because God's gifts put man's best dreams
    to shame.

My own Belovèd, who hast lifted me

From this drear flat of earth where I was
thrown,

And, in betwixt the languid ringlets, blown

A life-breath, till the forehead hopefully

Shines out again, as all the angels see,

Before thy saving kiss! My own, my own,

Who camest to me when the world was
gone,

And I who looked for only God, found *thee*!

XXVII

I find thee; I am safe, and strong, and glad.

As one who stands in dewless asphodel

Looks backward on the tedious time he had

In the upper life,—so I, with bosom-swell,

Make witness, here, between the good and
bad,

That Love, as strong as Death, retrieves as
well.

y letters! all dead paper, . . . mute and white!

And yet they seem alive and quivering

Against my tremulous hands which loose the string

And let them drop down on my knee to-night.

This said, . . . he wished to have me in his sight

Once, as a friend: this fixed a day in spring

To come and touch my hand. . . a simple thing,

Yet I wept for it!—this, . . . the paper's light . . .

XXVIII

Said, *Dear, I love thee*; and I sank and quailed
As if God's future thundered on my past.
This said, *I am thine*—and so its ink has paled
With lying at my heart that beat too fast.
And this . . .O Love, thy words have ill
    availed
If, what this said, I dared repeat at last!

 think of thee!—my thoughts do twine and bud

About thee, as wild vines, about a tree,

Put out broad leaves, and soon there's nought to see

Except the straggling green which hides the wood.

Yet, O my palm-tree, be it understood

I will not have my thoughts instead of thee

Who art dearer, better! Rather instantly

Renew thy presence; As a strong tree should,

XXIX

Rustle thy boughs and set thy trunk all
    bare,

And let these bands of greenery which in-
    sphere thee

Drop heavily down, . . . burst, shattered,
    everywhere!

Because, in this deep joy to see and hear
    thee

And breathe within thy shadow a new air,

I do not think of thee—I am too near thee.

F see thine image through my tears
 to-night,
And yet to-day I saw thee smiling. How
Refer the cause?—Belovèd, is it thou
Or I, who makes me sad? The acolyte
Amid the chanted joy and thankful rite
May so fall flat, with pale insensate brow,
On the altar-stair. I hear thy voice and vow,
Perplexed, uncertain, since thou art out of
 sight,

XXX

As he, in his swooning ears, the choir's
    Amen.

Belovèd, dost thou love? or did I see all

The glory as I dreamed, and fainted when

Too vehement light dilated my ideal,

For my soul's eyes? Will that light come
    again,

As now these tears come . . . falling hot and
    real?

Thou comest! all is said without a
word.

I sit beneath thy looks, as children do

In the noon-sun, with souls that tremble
through

Their happy eyelids from an unaverred

Yet prodigal inward joy. Behold, I erred

In that last doubt! and yet I cannot rue

The sin most, but the occasion . . . that we
two

Should for a moment stand unministered

XXXI

By a mutual presence. Ah, keep near and
    close,

Thou dovelike help! and, when my fears
    would rise,

With thy broad heart serenely interpose:

Brood down with thy divine sufficiencies

These thoughts which tremble when bereft
    of those,

Like callow birds left desert to the skies.

The first time that the sun rose on thine oath

To love me, I looked forward to the moon

To slacken all those bonds which seemed too soon

And quickly tied to make a lasting troth.

Quick-loving hearts, I thought, may quickly loathe;

And, looking on myself, I seemed not one

For such man's love!—more like an out-of-tune

Worn viol, a good singer would be wroth

XXXII

To spoil his song with, and which, snatched
   in haste,

Is laid down at the first ill-sounding note.

I did not wrong myself so, but I placed

A wrong on *thee.* For perfect strains may
   float

'Neath master-hands, from instruments
   defaced,—

And great souls, at one stroke, may do and
   doat.

*Y*es, call me by my pet-name! let me hear

The name I used to run at, when a child,

From innocent play, and leave the cowslips piled,

To glance up in some face that proved me dear

With the look of its eyes. I miss the clear

Fond voices which, being drawn and reconciled

Into the music of Heaven's undefiled,

Call me no longer. Silence on the bier,

XXXIII

While I call God...call God!—So let thy
    mouth

Be heir to those who are now exanimate.

Gather the north flowers to complete the
    south,

And catch the early love up in the late.

Yes, call me by that name,—and I, in truth,

With the same heart, will answer and not
    wait.

*W*ith the same heart, I said, I'll answer thee

As those, when thou shalt call me by my name—

Lo, the vain promise! is the same, the same,

Perplexed and ruffled by life's strategy?

When called before, I told how hastily

I dropped my flowers or brake off from a game,

To run and answer with the smile that came

At play last moment, and went on with me

XXXIV

Through my obedience. When I answer
    now,

I drop a grave thought, break from solitude;

Yet still my heart goes to thee . . . ponder
    how . . .

Not as to a single good, but all my good!

Lay thy hand on it, best one, and allow

That no child's foot could run fast as this
    blood.

*F*f I leave all for thee, wilt thou exchange

And be all to me? Shall I never miss

Home-talk and blessing and the common kiss

That comes to each in turn, nor count it strange,

When I look up, to drop on a new range

Of walls and floors, another home than this?

Nay, wilt thou fill that place by me which is

Filled by dead eyes too tender to know change?

XXXV

That's hardest. If to conquer love, has tried,

To conquer grief, tries more, as all things
prove;

For grief indeed is love and grief beside.

Alas, I have grieved so I am hard to love.

Yet love me—wilt thou? Open thine heart
wide,

And fold within the wet wings of thy dove.

*W*hen we met first and loved, I did not build

Upon the event with marble. Could it mean

To last, a love set pendulous between

Sorrow and sorrow? Nay, I rather thrilled,

Distrusting every light that seemed to gild

The onward path, and feared to overlean

A finger even. And, though I have grown serene

And strong since then, I think that God has willed

XXXVI

A still renewable fear. . .O love, O troth. . .

Lest these enclasped hands should never
    hold,

This mutual kiss drop down between us
    both

As an unowned thing, once the lips being
    cold.

And Love, be false! if *he*, to keep one oath,

Must lose one joy, by his life's star foretold.

*P*ardon, oh, pardon, that my soul should make,

Of all that strong divineness which I know

For thine and thee, an image only so

Formed of the sand, and fit to shift and break.

It is that distant years which did not take

Thy sovranty, recoiling with a blow,

Have forced my swimming brain to undergo

Their doubt and dread, and blindly to forsake

XXXVII

Thy purity of likeness and distort

Thy worthiest love to a worthless
    counterfeit:

As if a shipwrecked Pagan, safe in port,

His guardian sea-god to commemorate,

Should set a sculptured porpoise, gills
    a-snort

And vibrant tail, within the temple-gate.

*F*irst time he kissed me, he but only kissed

The fingers of this hand wherewith I write;

And, ever since, it grew more clean and white, . . .

Slow to world-greeting, quick with its 'Oh, list,'

When the angels speak. A ring of amethyst

I could not wear here, plainer to my sight,

Than that first kiss. The second passed in height

The first, and sought the forehead, and half missed,

XXXVIII

Half falling on the hair. O beyond meed!

That was the chrism of love, which love's
    own crown,

With sanctifying sweetness, did precede.

The third upon my lips was folded down

In perfect, purple state; since when,
    indeed,

I have been proud and said, 'My love, my
    own.'

*B*ecause thou hast the power and own'st the grace

To look through and behind this mask of me

(Against which years have beat thus blanchingly

With their rains), and behold my soul's true face,

The dim and weary witness of life's race,—

Because thou hast the faith and love to see,

Through that same soul's distracting lethargy,

The patient angel waiting for a place

XXXIX

In the new Heavens,—because nor sin nor
    woe,

Nor God's infliction, nor death's
    neighbourhood,

Nor all which others viewing, turn to go,

Nor all which makes me tired of all, self-
    viewed, . . .

Nothing repels thee, . . . Dearest, teach me
    so

To pour out gratitude, as thou dost, good!

h, yes! they love through all this world of ours!

I will not gainsay love, called love forsooth.

I have heard love talked in my early youth,

And since, not so long back but that the flowers

Then gathered, smell still. Mussulmans and Giaours

Throw kerchiefs at a smile, and have no ruth

For any weeping. Polypheme's white tooth

Slips on the nut if, after frequent showers,

XL

The shell is over-smooth,—and not so
    much

Will turn the thing called love, aside to hate

Or else to oblivion. But thou art not such

A lover, my Belovèd! thou canst wait

Through sorrow and sickness, to bring
    souls to touch,

And think it soon when others cry 'Too
    late.'

thank all who have loved me in their hearts,

With thanks and love from mine. Deep thanks to all

Who paused a little near the prison-wall

To hear my music in its louder parts

Ere they went onward, each one to the mart's

Or temple's occupation, beyond call.

But thou, who, in my voice's sink and fall

When the sob took it, thy divinest Art's

XLI

Own instrument didst drop down at thy
    foot,

To hearken what I said between my
    tears, . . .

Instruct me how to thank thee! Oh, to
    shoot

My soul's full meaning into future years,

That *they* should lend it utterance, and
    salute

Love that endures, from Life that
    disappears!

y future will not copy fair my past'—
I wrote that once; and thinking at my side
My ministering life-angel justified
The word by his appealing look upcast
To the white throne of God, I turned at last,
And there, instead, saw thee, not unallied
To angels in thy soul! Then I, long tried
By natural ills, received the comfort fast,

XLII

While budding, at thy sight, my pilgrim's
    staff

Gave out green leaves with morning dews
    impearled.

I seek no copy now of life's first half:

Leave here the pages with long musing
    curled,

And write me new my future's epigraph,

New angel mine, unhoped for in the world!

ow do I love thee? Let me count
the ways.

I love thee to the depth and breadth and
height

My soul can reach, when feeling out of
sight

For the ends of Being and ideal Grace.

I love thee to the level of everyday's

Most quiet need, by sun and candlelight.

I love thee freely, as men strive for Right;

I love thee purely, as they turn from Praise.

XLIII

I love thee with the passion put to use

In my old griefs, and with my childhood's
faith.

I love thee with a love I seemed to lose

With my lost saints,—I love thee with the
breath,

Smiles, tears, of all my life!—and, if God
choose,

I shall but love thee better after death.

Belovèd, thou hast brought me many flowers

Plucked in the garden, all the summer through

And winter, and it seemed as if they grew

In this close room, nor missed the sun and showers.

So, in the like name of that love of ours,

Take back these thoughts which here un-folded too,

And which on warm and cold days I withdrew

From my heart's ground. Indeed, those beds and bowers

XLIV

Be overgrown with bitter weeds and rue,

And wait thy weeding; yet here's eglantine,

Here's ivy!—take them, as I used to do

Thy flowers, and keep them where they
    shall not pine.

Instruct thine eyes to keep their colours
    true,

And tell thy soul their roots are left in mine.

Running Press Miniature Editions

This book has been bound using handcraft methods, and Smythe-sewn to ensure durability.

The dust jacket was designed by Toby Schmidt and illustrated by Pat Perleberg. The interior was designed and illustrated by Judith Barbour Osborne. The text was typeset in Weiss by Commcor Communications Corporation, Philadelphia, Pennsylvania.